W9-CDK-296

WALLABIES
AND **BABIES**
THEIR

MARIANNE JOHNSTON

A Zoo Life Book

The Rosen Publishing Group's
PowerKids Press™
New York

THE WALLABY

The wallaby is a furry animal that is closely related to the kangaroo. Wallabies hop around using their strong hind legs. And, like kangaroos, wallabies are **marsupials** (mar-SOO-pee-ulz). Marsupials carry their young in a pouch, or a fold of skin, on the front of their bodies. There are 60 different **species** (SPEE-sheez) of marsupials. Fifteen of those are different types of wallabies. If you visit Australia, New Guinea, or Tasmania, you can see these gentle, shy creatures in their natural **habitat** (HA-bih-tat). But many wallabies live in zoos throughout the world. And zoos all over the United States **raise** (RAYZ) wallabies.

ORDER:
MARSUPIALIA
FAMILY:
MACROPODIDAE

A wallaby, like this Bennett's wallaby, uses its strong tail for balance.

MANY DIFFERENT WALLABIES

One of the fifteen species of wallaby is the yellow-footed rock wallaby. Yellow-footed rock wallabies live in the rocky, dry areas of southern Australia. The fur on the feet of these wallabies is yellow or bright orange. Yellow-footed rock wallabies grow to be about three and a half feet long from head to tail. The northern nailtail wallaby lives in the northern parts of Australia. These wallabies have a small, fingernail-like tip at the end of their tails. Scientists aren't sure exactly how this "nail" is used. The parma wallaby is found only in a small area on the east coast of Australia. You can see many of the different species of wallabies at zoos.

Wallabies don't eat meat. Grass is a wallaby's favorite food. ▶

MARSUPIAL BABIES

Wallabies, like all marsupials, have pouches. Baby wallabies are raised inside these pouches. A human baby spends nine months growing inside a mother's body. After birth, the baby can **survive** (ser-VYV) outside of the mother's body.

Marsupials are different. Before a marsupial can survive outside the mother's body, a baby goes through two growth stages. The first stage takes place before birth. A baby marsupial spends a month growing inside its mother's body. Then the baby spends the second stage inside the mother's pouch.

A mother wallaby usually gives birth to only one baby at a time.

A baby wallaby grows more in the mother's pouch than in her belly.

WHEN A WALLABY IS BORN

After a month inside the mother's body, a wallaby is born. At birth, wallabies are smaller than your pinkie finger. They are blind and almost helpless.

Just before the birth, the mother wallaby will spend ten to fifteen minutes licking her own belly. The mother is making a trail with her **saliva** (suh-LY-vuh). After birth, the baby wallaby will crawl along the saliva trail to its mother's pouch. At this stage, the newborn looks more like a worm than a wallaby.

As it grows, a wallaby starts to look more like its mother. The baby grows fur and long back legs. ▶

INSIDE THE POUCH

A mother wallaby has **teats** (TEETS) inside her pouch. This is how the baby wallaby will drink the mother's milk after it has climbed up the mother's belly and into the pouch. The baby wraps its mouth around the teat. This is the wallaby's first drink of its mother's milk.

The amount of time a wallaby spends inside the mother's pouch is different for every type of wallaby. The yellow-footed rock wallaby leaves its mother's pouch at four to five weeks. The tammar wallaby leaves its mother's pouch at 36 weeks.

Like most wallabies, a parma wallaby has four teats inside its pouch.

WALLABIES AT THE ZOO

It is easy to tell when a human is **pregnant** (PREG-nunt). A pregnant woman's belly grows very large.

With wallabies, it's not as easy to tell. Wallabies don't get big bellies. And a baby wallaby, or **joey** (JOH-wee), is too small for people to see as it climbs up its mother's belly to the pouch.

Often zookeepers won't know that a wallaby was pregnant until after a joey is already inside the mother's pouch! There is one sign that a wallaby has had a baby. Sometimes there may be a little bit of blood on or near the mother from when the joey was born.

It is a very exciting time at a zoo when a baby wallaby is born. ▶

THE FIRST FEW DAYS

If zookeepers think a wallaby has had a baby, they will watch her closely. Zookeepers might notice that the mother is **grooming** (GROO-ming) her pouch. The wallaby does this by opening up her pouch with her hands and licking all around inside it. When she does this, she is making sure the baby and the pouch are clean. Even if the zookeepers see a female licking her pouch, they will not go near the mother to see if there's a joey. Wallabies can get very nervous and excited when they have a joey in their pouch. If a mother wallaby gets too excited, she might not be able to make the milk the joey needs to grow. This is why zookeepers leave the mother alone.

◀ Some wallabies stamp their feet when they get scared.

GROWING UP AT THE ZOO

Mother wallabies and their joeys don't get special care from zookeepers unless they need it. The mother and baby stay with the other wallabies, just as they do at other times. As a joey gets older, it will start to peek out of the mother's pouch. The joey wants to see what is going on outside.

Usually it takes six to eight months before a baby wallaby leaves the pouch completely. Even then, the young wallaby will stay outside for only a very short time.

Young wallabies get scared easily. They prefer the safety of the pouch. ▶

BECOMING INDEPENDENT

As time goes by, a joey will spend more and more time outside the pouch. A baby wallaby will start to **explore** (ek-SPLOR) the outside world. Soon a joey will even try eating solid food, such as lettuce or carrots.

By the time a joey is about ten months old, it is usually ready to be outside of its mother's pouch all the time. A joey will still stay close to its mother. But now the young wallaby is starting to **socialize** (SOH-shul-eyz) with the other wallabies. At one year, a wallaby is completely **independent** (in-dee-PEN-dent). A young wallaby doesn't need its mother's milk anymore. It can take care of itself.

The smaller wallaby in this picture was raised by zookeepers.

HUMANS RAISING A JOEY

Sometimes a mother wallaby can run out of milk for her joey. Or she may become sick. When this happens, zookeepers raise the joey themselves. Zookeepers become the joey's new parents. They might put the joey in a homemade pouch made from old shirts. Then the keeper will place a heating pad inside the pouch to make it warm and cozy for the joey. The keepers feed the joey milk made to taste just like its mother's milk. If everything goes well, the joey will become a healthy adult wallaby. The wallaby can then return to live with the other wallabies at the zoo.

WEB SITE

You can learn more about wallabies at this Web site: http://www.intertex.net/users/rzu2u/wallabies.htm

GLOSSARY

explore (ek-SPLOR) To look around at one's surroundings.

grooming (GROO-ming) When an animal or person cleans herself or himself.

habitat (HA-bih-tat) The surroundings where an animal lives.

independent (in-dee-PEN-dent) Thinking for and taking care of oneself.

joey (JOH-wee) A baby wallaby.

marsupial (mar-SOO-pee-ul) An animal that gives birth to babies that may be carried in the mother's pouch.

pregnant (PREG-nunt) When a female has a baby or babies growing inside her.

raise (RAYZ) To bring up a baby.

saliva (suh-LY-vuh) A liquid in a wallaby's mouth that helps to break up food.

socialize (SOH-shul-eyz) To seek out the company of others.

species (SPEE-sheez) A group of animals that are very much alike.

survive (ser-VYV) To keep living.

teat (TEET) The part of a female wallaby's body from where her baby drinks milk.

INDEX